THE REAL ESTATE BUYER'S GUIDE TO BUYING A HOUSE

Everything You Need to Know About Buying Your Home, From the Mind of a Successful Real Estate Professional

By

CAL KNECHT

GRI®, ABR®, SRS®, MRP®, SFR®, B.A.

This book is dedicated to my wife Arrí, as I would have never been able to have started and continued this journey in real estate without her continuous support.

I love you. You are always my forever.

Table of Contents

Introduction

Considering buying a home, but don't know where to start? You've come to the right place. First and foremost, congratulations on seeking assistance to aide in this stressful and time-consuming process. Second, you can push those jitters aside. Owning a home is the dream of many individuals around the world, and while it sounds like a scary process, if done correctly it will allow you to reap the rewards for years to come.

This book will walk you through every step of buying a home, holding your hand from the initial phases of obtaining and explaining potential loan options to working with an agent to closing on the property. The following pages will clearly identify things you need to do to prepare to purchase your new home as well as things to look out for along the way. This information will help you grow confident in your decision to buy a home as well as assist you in better understanding the often-complicated process.

As a Realtor® and real estate professional who has worked with countless clients from all walks of life, I have had the luxury to personally assist many people through the home-buying process and advise them on ways to protect their investment. This position has allowed me to obtain unique insight on common worries and frequently asked questions of first-time home buyers, as well as help provide guidance on perilous mistakes that I frequently see buyers make that end up being detrimental to them.

Before I worked in real estate, I was an Infantry Officer in the U.S. Army who moved several times and knew very little about the home-buying process. This left me and many of my fellow Soldiers in the dark about how to go about buying a home, making poor financial decisions throughout the process.

This book acts as a medium for me to further assist more individuals to make more informed decisions on what is typically the largest investment of their lives. The sooner you start reading, the faster you will be on your way to making an educated decision and protecting that investment.

Turn the page to start your journey to home ownership!

PART I:

One Small Step to Future Success

Chapter One:

Before You Step into The Arena

So, I hear you're interested in buying a home. Well, that's all fine and dandy. But what type of home are you looking for? What does your financial situation look like? Are there any special circumstances that are going on in your life? How much work are you willing to put in? Have any skills in a particular trade?

These are all questions that, while mundane, need to be at the forefront of your mind. At any given point in time, there are literally *millions* of homes available for sale all over the world. And they can range from a $3,500 burnt-down shack to a $40M mansion on 90 acres of land. So, if you start the conversation with just "Hey, I hate renting and want a house!" and don't follow it with much, that unfortunately is the equivalent to going car shopping and not knowing if you want a Lamborghini or a truck that doesn't run.

The very first thing that you, a potential home-owner, must do in order to make your dream a reality is sit down and go over your finances. How much do you have saved? Do you have any stocks, bonds, or investments you can cash in? How much can you afford to comfortably pay for a mortgage every month without drastically changing your current lifestyle? Have you paid off your credit cards? Are you behind on any payments? What's your credit score?

These questions are crucial in order for you to start off on the best foot possible. Buying a home, while not always, can require spending a sizable chunk of money for things that most people aren't familiar with that are a part of the home buying process. But don't let that scare you off, these items are necessary to protect you and your investment. We will get to those later on. For now, what we care about is getting a financial picture in order to have a foundation to build upon down the road.

In your financial picture, set it up just like a budget. It can be basic, it's just for your own knowledge. Track how much money you have coming in, and how much you have going out. Start with fixed expenses that don't change (rent, Wi-Fi, car payment, etc.) and then track your expenses that fluctuate (entertainment, dining out, etc.). From there, look to see how much you net from subtracting expenses from income. Pretty easy!

Now, you may work with the numbers a bit, and I know it sounds basic. You are always welcome to make it more advanced and detailed, of course. But the main purpose of this exercise is so you have some sort of framework as to how much leeway you have in affording a monthly mortgage payment. This will ultimately drive your property search, as it will allow you to target properties that you can realistically afford.

The single biggest mistake I see happen consistently in a transaction is people buying a property that is way out of their budget. As I will mention now and will mention once we talk about loans later on in this book, just because the lender gives you the ability to purchase up to a certain amount doesn't mean that you actually should. Think of it this way: just because you *can* eat a tub of ice cream doesn't mean that it is best for you to eat more than a few scoops in one sitting. Real estate works the same way. Spend more than you can afford, and you will regret it later. Don't say I didn't warn you.

After you have your financial picture in place, you need to be aware of your credit score. If you don't know your credit score, look it up! There are free apps like Credit Karma that can give you a rough ballpark of where it's at. Credit card companies often provide access to your FICO® score as well on their sites. This is an important number that will ultimately be the key to your success.

Your credit score is so important because it needs to be at a certain level in order to have the opportunity to obtain a loan. This is because your credit score helps determine to a lender how likely they are to receive payment from you for advancing a large sum of money for the purchase of property. At the time of this writing, I would recommend shooting for at least a 620 in order to have a reasonable chance at qualifying for a loan. If your credit score isn't there yet, work on it by consistently paying your bills on time and paying down your debts. This will help increase your score and eventually will allow you to purchase the home you desire. Talking to a loan officer can help give you an idea of what must be paid off in order to better increase your credit score as well.

The next item you must figure out is what you need in a home. Things to write down to narrow the search would be location, deal breakers (fenced yard, garage, etc.), number of bedrooms/bathrooms, and the size of the home. Then, at the very top of this piece of paper, write your monthly budget extremely large so you don't forget what is most important in the property search. This will help to set the framework for you to begin your search.

Now that you have these things in order, we can proceed to the next portion of the process: finding an agent and understanding agency relationships.

Chapter Summary/Key Takeaways

- Know your financial picture
- Put constraints on your search
- Wants vs. Needs
- Credit Score!!
- Don't miss payments

Chapter Two:

Selecting Your Corner

You're about to get into arguably the largest
financial transaction of your life. Butterflies are swarming
by the dozen inside of you, and you're anxious to find the
home of your dreams. You've been catching up on HGTV
re-runs of people flipping houses so you know the lingo,
and you're absolutely sure that you are ready to analyze
every portion of a potential home under a microscope.

Well, I've got some news for you: that's all
television voodoo magic. In real life, none of these things
happen. And I can guarantee that whatever agent took that
phone call or showed you that house is laughing about the
asinine thing someone did at their most recent showing
over a cup of coffee.

We all have stories like this. One of my favorites
is a guy calling me trying to buy a move-in ready four-
bedroom home in a swanky neighborhood offering to pay
$10K cash. One of my first calls I ever received in the
business was a woman with a horrific credit score and
$500 of monthly income trying to convince me to sell her
a $400K house because she saw it happen on a tv show.
And the list goes on. Ask any real estate professional and
they could tell you a tremendous number of stories of
clueless people getting mad at them because of something

they saw on television. The purpose of this chapter is to provide an in-depth analysis on to how not to be that guy.

To start yourself off on the right path to homeownership success, you *need* to have a *good* **agent**. I repeat. *Good. Agent.* You are a novice, and you need the guidance of an established industry professional to help lead the way. So how can you figure out who is reputable and who to shy away from? How can you get in touch with an agent in the first place?

Let's start here. If you called asking for property information on Zillow, Realtor.com, Trulia, or any of the major real estate websites, this is what happens: the call is routed to a local agent that pays for leads in that zip code. That's it. While qualified to help, that individual most likely has never stepped foot on or near whatever property you called about asking for more information on. If you see that 123 Main St in Anywhere, Alabama is a 3 bed 2 bath listed at $150K on 2.5 acres and is 1780 square feet, guess what? That is the exact same information they have in front of their screen. Unless they happen to be the listing agent, they weren't the ones that wrote the listing, and have never met the seller in most cases. And if you ask for more pictures, you won't get any because they didn't take them. The listing agent did.

So now you think, "Ah, so I must speak with the listing agent!" Not necessarily. In my personal opinion, that generally is the single worst decision you can make in the entire home-buying process. What you want to do is interview real estate professionals and find one that is knowledgeable about laws, loans, and the area. It also is a plus if they're friendly and you feel comfortable working with them. But remember this: *it is generally NOT in your best interest as a buyer to work with the listing agent!*

Let's break down agency in a nutshell.

1. **Agency** is the term used to describe the formal relationship a potential buyer/seller has with a real estate professional. 2. There are many types of agency relationships. 3. These relationships are formed in written documentation. 4. Not all agency relationships protect your best interests as a buyer.

When it comes to buying a property, you want someone who's sole interest is in protecting your investment and getting you the best deal possible on the best property available. This is why you need representation, because let's be honest: you wouldn't be reading this if you knew everything about real estate. But furthermore, a real estate agent that you have an agency relationship with can help ensure you don't fall prey to the perils of cleverly worded contracts and hidden details that you would most likely overlook as someone who doesn't conduct transactions on a daily basis.

Which leads us back to why you don't want to work with the listing agent. The reason why, as a buyer, you don't want to work with the listing agent is because they have a signed listing agreement WITH THE SELLER binding them to treat the seller as a client and put their needs first. Therefore, you become a customer INSTEAD OF becoming a client, causing what can be a conflict of interest.

This conflict of interest hurts you and only you because the listing agent knows how much the seller will take for the property, and is listening to your every word to potentially counter the offer you will make and get a better deal for the seller, NOT for you as the buyer. And you willingly signed up for that if you choose this method. Don't get mad at the agent, they are following the law and doing their job, you were the one silly enough to think they had your best interest at heart.

Dual agency is a situation that can arise as well. Let's say that you were working with an agent and they happen to be the listing agent of a home that you are interested in. Well, there are two options. First, you and the seller can both agree to be represented by the same agent. This will be in writing, and only can happen if state laws allow dual agency. Second, you can ask to work with a **designated agent**.

A designated agent in these scenarios is someone that is assigned to work with you to protect your interests. Usually within the same brokerage, it becomes this person's duty to protect your interests and negotiate in your behalf to protect you and your interests.

In my opinion, the smart thing for you to do in a situation like the one above is to find an established agent that you have good rapport with and sign a buyer brokerage agreement with them. This is a document that solidifies your agency relationship with that individual, making them put your interests first over another individuals. In exchange, it says that you will be loyal to them and will allow them to represent you throughout the transaction. And this documentation grounded with loyalty is the keystone when it comes to building your corner.

When looking for an established agent, feel free to interview several. Just don't expect them to do free work. Anytime an individual says they are working with multiple agents, that is not someone the vast majority of agents will want to deal with. Why? Because if you approach me and say that, I will say that I appreciate the opportunity however I have other clients who I've formed a mutual loyalty with that want to be assisted by me, and I won't spend time working for someone that isn't willing to let me help them without worrying that I won't be able to feed my family for all those hours I put in.

So, you may ask, what is a good agent, and how does one go about finding a good agent? A good agent has connections with great loan officers, a slew of contractors, and knows everyone you will ever need for any issue you may come across in the home-buying process. Their job is to literally take care of you and hold your hand throughout the entirety of the transaction to make it as stress-free as possible. Need a termite letter? Taken care of. Recommendations for a home inspector? I know a guy. Need the septic tank cleaned and inspected? Too easy.

And the list can get extensive, from arborists to soil specialists to surveyors and everything in between.

The quality of service is what separates the good agents from the ones that need improvement. Even in transactions, I have worked with some agents on the other side that make you wonder how they still have clients in the first place because of how poorly they've represented them in contracts and advising their clients in what to ask for in repairs. (Side note – as a buyer using a mortgage, *never* ask for rotten wood to be replaced after your home inspection. It will come up as a necessary repair when the appraiser comes to the property). On the flip side, the great agents will have made the transaction a breeze for the other agent involved, taking care of not only their client but ensuring that all documentation has been correctly completed and filed with the appropriate attorneys, loan originators, underwriters, and contractors involved in the transaction.

A good agent will serve you with pleasure and will ensure that you are always being taken care of every step of the way, and they will also advise you if you start to get a bit carried away. Case in point, a client couldn't fathom purchasing a beautiful $468K home because "her $1K dining room table didn't fit." She walked away from what was the perfect home to her spouse's surprise because of such a silly detail. Days later, after her spouse convinced her that they could easily afford a new, nicer dining room table, the house had already sold to someone that realized they could buy 468 dining room tables for the same price as the house. This is why your agent is there. They will politely give you a reality check to help protect your best interests.

Once you have a strong agent in your corner, let them help you. Feel free to ask questions, but don't overstep your boundaries. That individual has a lot more expertise than you do and will ensure you are taken care of. If they tell you something, it's coming from experience. Remember, real estate agents are only paid by commission, and if they're successful, it's because they have a LOT of experience buying and selling properties.

One big thing to keep in mind as we transition: if you ever do come across a situation where you have an issue with an agent, talk it out. Speak with them. Odds are it's a minor miscommunication. But under ZERO circumstances should you as a buyer say anything along the lines of "What am I paying you for?" or "Why aren't you doing X? You're working for me; I'm telling you what to do!" Why? Because in most cases, the SELLER pays the commission, not the buyer. So, therefore, you aren't paying your agent anything as a buyer. 2. Real estate agents, unless a brokerage has otherwise noted, are independent contractors and therefore they do NOT work for you. At any point in time a real estate agent can (although very rarely) fire you as a client. I personally have fired three clients in my career, and while it is not a frequent thing and not something I try to do, I will not tolerate racism/hate/intolerance, breaking laws, general rudeness, or micromanagement.

The last thing to remember: while a good agent will do everything they can to make you feel important, you *are not* the only client they have. Agents make their own hours and juggle multiple transactions and their family lives. I can tell you that I work over 100 hours a week, 7 days a week, and try to spend any free minute I have with my family. So please, while agents do thoroughly enjoy assisting you, just remember that if you've called us three times within a two hour span on a Sunday morning just to chat about houses you may or may not be interested in seeing, and you have an appointment booked for the following afternoon, please be cognizant about why you are calling. Your agent will thank you for it and will gladly assist you even more so if they don't consistently receive phone calls at 11:30 pm to talk about properties you saw on Zillow.

Ultimately, and just like in every industry, there are great individuals and there are those that are less than stellar. Find someone that is good at what they do and that jives well with you. Your corner is one of the most critical components of creating a successful transaction. Ensure to take your time and figure out what will work best for you.

Chapter Summary/Key Takeaways

- Find an agent that is right for you
- Do your research

Knecht/The Real Estate Buyer's Guide to Buying A House

- Know what agency relationship you have
- Be flexible
- Trust your agent

Knecht/The Real Estate Buyer's Guide to Buying A House

Chapter Three:

Finding the Right Mortgage for You

Just like there are many home options available for you to consider, there are many mortgages programs at your disposal. If you do not have the funds available to purchase your property in cold hard cash, a mortgage may be something that you want to consider to help you obtain your dream home.

Mortgages come in various shapes and sizes. Different programs require different down payments, some have different interest rates, and some have different term lengths. The following information is to give you an idea about options that may be of interest to consider in your home-buying process. For full loan details and options, I'd recommend speaking with a licensed loan officer.

VA Loans

If you are in the U.S. military or are an honorably discharged veteran, you have the ability to utilize the VA Loan Program. This program is an awesome opportunity should you qualify for it. It provides the ability to purchase a property with down-payments as low as 0%, fixed-rates, and 30-year terms with no pre-payment penalty should you qualify. There are cases where you can have two active VA loans. Also, a little-known fact is that as long as your loans are continuously paid off, there is no limit to the amount of times you can utilize this program. For more information on the VA Loan Program, speak with a licensed loan officer.

USDA Loans

The USDA Loan Program is another great option to utilize if you and the property qualify for it. This program allows for properties located in certain areas outside of metropolitan areas in less urban settings to be obtained with as down-payments as low as 0%, fixed-rates, and 30-year terms with no pre-payment penalties. This loan is useful should you wish to move to a less populated area and not be required to put down a large amount of funds to secure financing. For more information on the USDA Loan Program and whether or not specific properties qualify for this mortgage option, speak with a licensed loan officer.

FHA Loans

The FHA Loan Program is a mortgage option that I see used very frequently. This mortgage option allows for you to obtain a mortgage for a property with down-payments as low as 3.5%, fixed-rates, and 30-year terms with no pre-payment penalties. This loan can be a great option if you want to obtain financing on a property, don't have a lot of funds saved, and cannot obtain a VA or USDA loan. For more information on the FHA Loan Program and whether it is right for you, speak with a licensed loan officer.

Conventional Loans

Conventional Loan Programs are an option that can be utilized to obtain properties if you have saved some money for a down-payment. The percentage changes, however, it typically requires a down-payment of at least 15% to 20% of the purchase price of the property. These loans allow for you as the buyer to typically obtain a lower monthly payment on the property. This is due to the lack of Private Mortgage Insurance when the loan balance drops below 80% of the purchase price of the property. This can be a good option to utilize if you have some available funds, want to buy a fixer-upper, or have borderline credit. For more information on Conventional Loan Programs and whether they are right for you, speak with a licensed loan officer.

Other Financing Options

Outside of the aforementioned mortgage programs, there are many other options that you may

consider to obtain financing on a property. Some states,
like Georgia, have programs that can help those who need
down-payment assistance with programs like Georgia
Dream. These are state programs and options may or may
not be available to you in the state you wish to purchase
property in.

Other options that may be available to you would
be hard-money lenders, investment loans, and other
unconventional options. These are all options that you
want to exercise caution while exploring, as the terms of
the loan vary and are not the same across the board. For
more information about state loan program options,
down-payment assistance, and unconventional financing
options speak with a licensed loan officer.

Closing Costs

When you obtain a mortgage, there is something
called closing costs that you will be responsible for
paying. These can be paid by the seller through the
negotiation phase while purchasing property, or it can be
paid in cash by you as the borrower. In certain scenarios,
the funds can be gifted to you by a family member.

Closing costs are the items required to be paid in
order for the mortgage to be obtained and for the attorney
to transfer ownership of the property from the seller to the
buyer. From mortgage origination fees to document
preparation fees, there are many costs that you will incur

when obtaining a mortgage to finance a property. The thing to keep in mind is that you are responsible for these costs, and they need to be paid prior to your loan being funded. Regardless of what mortgage program you choose to utilize, there will be costs associated with the loan that you should be prepared to pay. To learn more about closing costs, speak with a licensed loan officer.

Chapter Summary/Key Takeaways

- Know the mortgage options available to you
- Find the right option for you
- Save for closing costs
- Speak with a licensed loan officer

PART II:

Finding the Right Property for You

Chapter Four:

Starting the Property Search

Searching for properties is the fun part of buying real estate, and it also can be a headache if you don't approach it properly. Your goal in this phase of buying property is to identify the home of your dreams. To effectively do this, there are a few things that need to be conducted in order to ensure you are successful in your search.

To reach your goal, it is not your objective to see as many properties as possible. If you are looking for a move-in ready starter home under $200,000 it is not in your best interest to see $500,000 mansions or $15,000 fixer-uppers. Just because a property is for sale does not mean it matches your needs. The following will provide some added insights to assist you during your search.

Narrowing It Down

In Chapter One, we created your budget to determine how much you can afford to pay monthly for your mortgage. With that in mind, talk with your lender about the amount you are pre-qualified for. Again, remember that just because you *can* buy up to a certain amount doesn't mean you should. Always keep your monthly payment amount in the forefront of your mind.

That said, this is the time that you can start getting a little picky. Take your wants versus needs chart to start the search. For example, narrow it down by stating you need a 3b/2ba home under $200,000 within a 30-minute commute to your office. Let's say that this narrows the search of properties down from 1,000 to 350. That is still a lot of properties, and there is no way you can walk through all 350 of them.

Now, included in the 350 properties are those that may need major repairs. So our next step to narrow things even more is to put a minimum purchase price of $100,000. Let's say that doing this leaves 125 properties available, which is still too many to tour.

Now let's say that you want at least one acre of land with a fenced back yard and a pool. This will further narrow your search down from 125 properties to 12. This is a lot more manageable, however there is still a little more filtering to do. For the final filter we will add, let's say that you want the master bedroom on the main floor. That will drop your results to 5 properties, which is much more manageable amount than the 1,000 we started with.

As you can see from the previous example, narrowing your search is a very important part of the search process. As you do filter things down, remember to not get too picky to the point where there aren't any properties that match your criteria. Don't expect to find a

5b/3ba house with a pool on five acres and in pristine condition for under $50,000 if the market in that area states that they typically sell for $300,000. While that is just an example, always remember that if you filter your search too much, you may not have any results. You can always add things to a property later after it is purchased.

What to Look For

Once you have narrowed down your search, it's time to make an appointment to see the property. Your agent will take care of scheduling the tour. While there, this is your window of opportunity to see everything that the property holds, so look closely. Pictures you saw online can be deceiving.

The first thing you want to look at is the terrain. Is it right against the road? Does it sit on a hill? Where will the water pool when it rains? Is it near a busy road or highway? These are just some of the things you will want to consider before determining if the property is right for you. Everybody has different opinions on what is important to them, so ensure that you determine what does and doesn't matter in regard to the landscape of the property.

Second, check out the exterior of the property. Are there cracks in the brick? Does anything look weathered? Are there gutters? How does the roof look? Does anything need to be painted? While no property is perfect, this will give you some idea prior to having a home inspection conducted of the amount of work the property requires.

Third, once you are in the house make sure to turn on the faucets, flush the toilets, turn on the lights, and check all the cabinets. Look for anything that needs to be painted or fixed. See if there could be evidence of a leak. Ultimately, you want to have an idea of the amount of money you will need to spend to make the property habitable prior to occupying it. Your home inspection will confirm these issues at a later date.

Take all of these potential issues into account when you do your pro-con chart on each of these properties. Also determine if you like the floorplan, the layout of the kitchen and master bedroom, as well as anything else that is important to you in your decision-making process. For each property you view, write everything down for future evaluation and comparison.

Chapter Summary/Key Takeaways

- Monthly Payment!!
- Wants vs. Needs
- Narrow it down
- Potential repairs
- Write down pros and cons

Chapter Five:

Comparing Properties

Comparing properties is one of the more challenging parts of the real estate process. Not only are you comparing features based on personal preference, you are also in the midst of assigning values to the features you are deciding whether or not you need. The comparison process is the phase that helps you determine what you want and your agent determine the value of the property in comparison to the sale of similar properties in the area. This is called a **Comparative Market Analysis**, or CMA for short. We will get into that in a minute. For now, let's start by looking at how to begin this phase.

Pros and Cons

The first step in the comparison phase is to take out the pro/con worksheets that you completed for each property. Lay them out next to each other and get three different markers; one green, one yellow, and one red. Using the markers, we are going to color-coordinate your pro/con worksheets to compare the specific properties that you viewed.

Take the green marker first and highlight all the important positives each property has. Continuing from our previous example where we filtered our search, let's say that you highlight all the properties that have privacy fencing instead of chain-link fencing. Then, let's say you highlight properties with granite countertops in the kitchen.

For any of the properties that don't have these features, you highlight that portion red. Use yellow for any property that is middle of the road. For the fencing example, you could highlight the fencing section yellow if a portion of it was privacy fencing and the rest chain-link. For the counter-tops, you could highlight it yellow if they were granite but they weren't your desired color. Anything section highlighted red would mean that the property lacked said feature.

Once you have all five of your worksheets color-coordinated, remove the two with the most red marks on them. This will leave you with your top three properties. Now, this is when you look at the amount of work the properties may potentially need. The amount of work often can sway what was your number one pick to be your number three.

For example, if you determine that you love property A but need to remove all the carpeting in the bedrooms, this is something that you need to consider. If property B has a different shade of granite countertops in the kitchen but has hardwood flooring throughout the house, this is something you will need to thoroughly consider. Something to keep in mind is whether or not the

color of your kitchen counters is worth having to
potentially spend thousands on replacing the carpets. You
may also decide that you are okay with having carpets in
the bedroom as well. These are just a small sample of the
decisions you will be faced with, some more important
than others.

Once you have completed this exercise, rank your
properties in order from one to three and give them to your
agent. This will be where they start comparing properties
to the market you are in to give you a better idea of the
valuation of those properties.

Comparative Market Analysis

For each of the three properties, your agent can
pull them up and balance them in comparison to recent
sales in the area. This will help to give a better
understanding on the pricing of the property in relation to
the current market. By doing this your agent can provide
you with property values and a range of what price they
expect the property to sell for. This ultimately gives you
as a buyer a better idea of what the property is worth prior
to submitting an offer.

A CMA in short compares a specific subject
property to other properties within a close proximity to the
subject that have sold recently. The properties will be
selected to be as similar to the subject property as possible
in size, age, bedrooms, bathrooms, acreage, and many

other criteria. Typically three to five comparable properties are chosen to give an accurate representation of the market, however your agent can use as many or as few as they see fit based on market conditions.

For each characteristic of the property, the agent will provide a value to adjust the comparable property to match the subject properties characteristics. For example, if the subject house is 2,000 square feet, and the comparable is 2,200 square feet, the agent will adjust accordingly based on a certain value. The goal is to manipulate the comparable property's sale price to be adjusted as if it were based on the characteristics of the subject property.

Once all comparable properties have been adjusted, they will be assigned weighted percentages. Properties in the same neighborhood will typically be weighted more heavily than those in subdivisions miles away. Curb appeal also plays a factor here as well. For example, a comparable property in a highly sought-after community with a HOA may be weighted differently if the subject property is on a busy main road than if the subject property is also in a similar community.

When all properties have been weighted accordingly, the overall adjusted prices of each property will be averaged based on their weighting. This will result in having a valuation of the property. This number will give both you and your agent an educated estimate of the subject property's value so you can prepare accordingly prior to submitting offers.

Once all three of your potential properties have their estimated valuations completed, s down and compare them again. Look at the differences in valuation for each property to see which properties may be overpriced and what property appeals to you most based on the financial picture they present and the pro/con worksheets you completed earlier. Re-order the properties again to decide your top two and remove the third from contention. The next step will be crafting and submitting offers!

Chapter Summary/Key Takeaways

- Highlight pros and cons

- Take a good look at necessary repairs

- Factor in property valuations

- Determine your top two properties

Chapter Six:

Crafting Offers

The most exciting part of the home-buying experience is the negotiation process. This is where you can get the home of your dreams if you negotiate like a champion. The key to remember here is that in real estate transactions, literally *everything* is negotiable and anything can happen. I've even seen a bass fishing trip negotiated into a deal before. I'm not kidding when I say anything can be incorporated into a negotiation. The real question is where to start.

You and your agent have, at this point, sat down and come up with estimated valuations for each property. While these numbers are good information, they are not concrete. You still need to be flexible on purchase price. But that still doesn't mean you have to pay list price, either. It all depends on what items are most important to you to obtain and what the seller is willing to give in exchange.

The Basics of the Offer

The first part of crafting an **offer** is to understand what options are available to be negotiated. To determine this, speak with your agent. Oftentimes, these options

aren't just the purchase price of the property. Things to
consider include how much closing costs you'd like the
seller to provide. If your knee-jerk reaction is to say, "I
want the seller to pay all my closing costs," that's fine.
However, understand that changes the price you will be
paying.

Picture this. You want to give me $100 for your
house. You also owe your friend $6. You say that you will
buy my house for the above price, as long as I pay your
friend the money you owe them. So essentially, you are
giving me $94 for my home. This basic math applies to
something that we spoke about earlier: closing costs!!

Remember how we said you will be required to
pay closing costs for your mortgage? This is where those
come into play. If you do not want to pay closing costs out
of pocket, the seller is able to pay them for you by having
them rolled into your mortgage via purchase price. This
gives you the option to buy the house at one price or
increase the price by the amount of closing costs you
require and offer that price instead. Ultimately, the
purpose of doing this is to protect you from needing funds
coming out of your pocket in order to close on the house
you are attempting to purchase.

Items You Can Ask For

As mentioned previously, all things can be
negotiated in an offer for real estate. There are many

things you may consider asking the seller to provide for
you with an accepted offer. These things can not only save
you headaches, but they can also provide potentially large
amounts of savings to you as a buyer. And many of these
items are things most people don't even realize are
available to them.

One thing you can ask the seller to provide you
with is a clear termite letter. This is a certificate given by
a pest control company that states whether there is or has
been an infestation in the property of any insect that can
cause harm to your property. The company looks for signs
of active and past infestations and puts together a report.
If the property comes back without signs of these insects,
they issue an official letter.

The costly part of this is when there is an issue. If
there is an infestation that needs to be treated, the cost to
treat and potentially repair any damage can be quite high.
If the seller agrees to provide a clear termite letter in the
contract, these costs will fall on them and not you as the
buyer.

Another item that may be worth asking for is a
home warranty. Home warranties vary from company to
company, but the gist of them is that while your property
is under one you pay a flat fee for them to send a
contractor out and fix the problem. These can be a great
thing to have because you are moving into a property and
things can happen. You may use the electrical or
plumbing different than the previous owner, and items

break all the time. This is one way to protect your investment at a lower cost than needing to fix things yourself. Obviously the warranty has limitations depending on the company providing it and the chosen plan, however it is something that can be useful to you as a buyer.

Some other things that could be worth asking for in your offer are HVAC inspections, having the chimney swept, pumping the septic tank, and anything else that you feel needs to be done. If the floors are worn, you may ask for a flooring allowance. No refrigerator? Ask for one! The only limitations you have are the ones you create for yourself. That said, and this is important, you are only *asking* that the seller provides these items for you. Nothing says they must provide them unless they agree to the terms of the contract.

If you ask for everything under the sun, chances are the seller is not going to do more than a few of the things you ask for in the offer. The more you ask for, the more it costs them in the deal. The seller typically has a budget for providing concessions that depends on the price being offered. It all depends on what they are willing to do and whether you crafted the offer efficiently.

Little things are not something you want to be asking for during this portion of the process. There will be time to ask for repairs later on. Right now you want to get the property under contract at a reasonable price and with your desired concessions from the seller. Nothing is stopping the seller from countering your offer or accepting a different offer. In several states, the seller doesn't even need to respond to your offer. The seller is human, too. If you really want that property, don't irritate them in the offers process by asking for too much. The good agent you are working with will tell you when you are starting to go overboard and bring you back to a more realistic offer. While you are always welcome to offer whatever you want, remember that they handle transactions for a living and have a better idea about what will be acceptable to a seller than you do in that particular market.

Once the offer has been put together and all the documents have been signed, the offer will be submitted to the listing agent to present to the seller. From there, you will either receive a counteroffer, be under contract, or have the offer declined. If there are multiple offers on the table, the seller may ask for "Highest and Best" in which they ask for all parties to submit their best offer for the property and go from there. Once the offer has been submitted, it becomes a waiting game.

If the seller provides a counteroffer, you can either accept the offer or counter the offer. This back and forth process can go on infinitely until both parties reach an agreement or decide to part ways. The good agent you are working with will not let this negotiation die as long as you tell them you want the property. If the seller or your expectations are not in line with the market, then you may need to look for a different property. If you end up under contract, then you will move on to the due diligence and inspection period, which we will cover in the next chapter.

Chapter Summary/Key Takeaways

- Determine amount of closing costs needed

- Remember basic mathematics

- Factor in concessions

- Keep negotiating until an agreement is reached

- Let your agent work to get you the best deal

PART III:

Is This the Right Home for You?

Chapter Seven:

The Due Diligence Process

Once you are under contract, the due diligence process begins. **Due diligence**, which may also be known as the inspection period, is the timeframe in a real estate contract that a buyer is allowed to conduct inspections on the property and gather any and all information that the buyer deems necessary in order to help them make a more educated purchase.

If, for whatever reason, the buyer decides to cancel the contract during the due diligence period, the buyer typically is refunded their **earnest money** and the contract is terminated. Should the buyer terminate the contract after the due diligence period has expired, alternative measures are taken. You can read more about some of the potential outcomes of these situations later on in the chapter.

Due Diligence in A Nutshell

The due diligence period is your best friend as a buyer. In the Purchase and Sale Agreement between the seller and yourself, the number of days in the due diligence period is negotiated. Day one of the due diligence process begins on the binding agreement date of the contract, unless otherwise noted.

As a buyer, your objective is to obtain as much information as possible about the property in this window of opportunity. While I am not saying to go overboard, I would urge you to learn as much as possible about the property and its surrounding area. This will give you a better scope of what to expect upon obtaining this specific property.

Examples of things you may wish to conduct or inquire about, in no particular order, are as follows:

Items to Potentially Consider Investigating During the Due Diligence Period

Home Inspection	Crime Statistics	Zoning	Traffic Counts	HOAs
School District	Flood Maps	Property Lines	Past Surveys	Wetlands
Covenants and Restrictions	Transit Schedules and Routes	Plans for Development	Conservation Programs	Other Desired Information

The aforementioned table is merely a few suggestions and is not meant to be a comprehensive list of items you may wish to conduct during this process. It is provided as a starting point to help exercise your mind while determining what is information you believe is important to know prior to completing the purchase of a property.

The process of inspecting a property is different between property classifications as well. For instance, a survey may serve as a better investment if you are building a new construction or are purchasing several acres of land and may not be of as much assistance if the property is in an established residential neighborhood. Ultimately, it is your decision on whether or not you wish to conduct a survey on a given property, however you may find that there are other ways to allocate those funds that may be more beneficial to you.

The Home Inspection

Home inspections are not a requirement to purchase a house. That said, they can be something that is highly encouraged depending on the terms of the contract and the property at hand. Generally speaking, a home inspection is encouraged as it can help the buyer understand more about the condition of the property and what repairs may need to be conducted.

A home inspection, when conducted by a *reputable* and *licensed* home inspector, can provide a wealth of knowledge and insight in regard to a property's condition. Home inspections tend to cover everything from plumbing fixtures and electrical wiring to the condition of the roof and appliances in the dwelling. They can tell you if the water heater is functioning properly and the general condition of the HVAC system. In short, they briefly touch a lot of bases in order to provide you with concrete evidence about the property itself.

While a home inspection is an expense that you will incur as a buyer, it generally is a worthy investment. It primarily allows for the buyer to do two things:

1. Determine what repairs, if any, the buyer wishes to ask the seller to conduct; or

2. Determine whether or not the buyer wishes to continue with the purchase of the property.

In the past, there have been home inspections that have come back on certain properties that I have had clients interested in purchasing that have shown the property to require significant repairs. Now, this is few and far between, but I always let my client know during this situation that I would rather they pay a few hundred dollars to avoid making what could be a bad investment instead of spending several hundred thousand dollars and being stuck with the property.

The reason why a home inspection is an important part of this process is because that report will delineate anything and everything that is worthy of your attention. That does not mean that the seller must or will fix any or

every item on that report; it simply allows you to be
cognizant of what the house may need repaired.

Requesting Repairs

The home inspection report leads us into the next
phase of the due diligence process: asking for repairs.
Utilizing the report provided by the home inspector, and
after sitting down with your real estate professional, you
will begin to decipher every reported problem that may
need to be addressed.

To caveat this, there will be a lot of minor items
noted on the report that should be taken with a grain of
salt. When compiling the repairs list that you wish the
seller to complete, the goal is to get the main items taken
care of. Anything that can potentially be pricey or "open
a can of worms" are the things to focus your attention on.
Keep the list reasonable and not too lengthy. Remember,
the seller is also operating on a budget too. If you begin to
ask the seller to replace the missing wall plates for the
light switches or the drain stoppers in the tub, you may
wish to reconsider your priorities.

Remember, you are only *asking* that the seller
repair these items. After you have finalized your list and
submit it to the seller, it is still a part of the negotiation.
The seller may agree to do all of them, they may cross off
a few of them and provide a counteroffer, or they may
state that they are selling the property as-is. The bottom

line is that your real estate professional will be there by your side, and their role is to work every angle and keep you informed on what is occurring every step of the way.

There are certain properties that you may not be able to ask for repairs on as well. In many cases, foreclosed REO/bank properties will not provide any repairs not required by the lender, if at all. These properties can typically be acquired for a lesser price than other similar properties in a different condition or status, however the negotiation process works differently. These properties at times can be a great investment if you are handy and do not mind putting sweat equity into the property.

Do Your Research

In my opinion, the most important thing that any buyer can do is extensively research any property that they are considering purchasing. Regardless of your experience level, whether you have never purchased property before or have been involved in hundreds of real estate transactions, I always am an advocate for doing the research. Even in the numerous transactions that I have been a party to, I am always learning something new every day. You never know what may emerge in a real estate transaction that seemed quite simple in the beginning. A property may turn out to be in a flood zone, someone else's name may be on the title from a previous transaction, the appraisal may determine that the property needs extensive repairs… These are only a few examples of the seemingly endless list of possibilities that may arise and need to be dealt with accordingly.

The only way to truly mitigate the risk involved in purchasing real estate, or anything for that matter, is by conducting adequate research. While it is impossible to know everything about a property, it definitely helps to know as much as possible. As a buyer, purchasing a home tends to be one of the largest transactions you will make in your lifetime, and as such it is imperative to do your homework. What you may not consider to be a problem now may turn into a major factor at a later date in the future.

As a real estate professional, there is no definitive way for me to tell you that the property you are purchasing will increase or diminish in value. While I do everything I can to ensure my clients are purchasing a solid investment, I have no control over the market and cannot stop the property appreciating or depreciating in value through the various booms and busts. That said, my goal and purpose is to ensure that you are making a purchase that makes you happy and can have some of the risk mitigated during the various market swings by maintaining your property and purchasing something that historically is a desirable property.

All in all, while your real estate professional will do everything they can to obtain as much information as possible about a specific property on your behalf, the most important concept to understand is to do your research. At the end of the day, you as the buyer will be the one responsible for the property's upkeep and maintenance, and everything that does or does not happen to said property is ultimately your responsibility. Because of this, I urge you to know what you are buying and understand both the pros and cons of each property you are considering before determining which home is right for you.

Chapter Summary/Key Takeaways

- Do your research!

- Know when the due diligence period ends

- Conduct a home inspection if desired/applicable

- Be smart when asking for repairs

- Refer to the first bullet!

Chapter Eight:

The Appraisal

Congratulations on making it this far! While we are starting to hit the tail end of the process of buying a home, we are not quite there yet. If you have opted to finance the purchase of a home, there is one hurdle remaining: the appraisal.

An **appraisal** is a document requested by a bank or lender which dictates the perceived value of a specific property. This is determined by an **appraiser** who checks the property for various hazards, code violations, and necessary repairs. The appraiser also conducts an analysis similar to the CMA's we spoke of in Chapter Five to help determine the value of the property in question.

The appraisal is a key part of the lending process because it determines what needs to be done in order to continue with the sale of a given property. The appraiser will provide the lender with a highly detailed report stating the valuation that they have given the property and any necessary repairs that must be conducted in order for the loan to be approved. The following are a few of the more common scenarios that may occur. For more information on the following and other possible outcomes, speak with a licensed loan officer.

The Appraisal Came Back "All Clear"

While relatively uncommon, it is possible for the appraisal report to state that the property value met or exceeded the purchase price agreed upon in the contract, and that no repairs are necessary in order to close. This is possible, although is generally presumed to be rare by many real estate professionals. If this happens, the property being purchased is in a small minority of real estate transactions from my past experience.

The House Appraised, But Needs Repairs

This result is far more common than the previous outcome. Put simply, the appraiser has determined that the property's valuation has met or exceeded the purchase price agreed upon in the contract, however certain items need to be fixed in order to secure funding. Although the appraiser can highlight many different defects, the more common items I have seen in past experience that need to be repaired or replaced are rotting wood, chipping paint, adjusting columns, and other relatively minor yet important defects. The financing amendment that was completed with the initial contract typically states that the seller is responsible for providing a specified amount towards lender required repairs. Any remaining repairs that the lender has deemed necessary to be completed prior to **closing** can be negotiated or paid for by the buyer. For more information on your specific transaction, speak with the licensed real estate professional you have been working with and speak with a licensed loan officer, as laws vary from state to state.

The Appraisal Came Back Short, And Repairs Are Needed

While frustrating, there are cases where the appraisal's valuation is below the amount agreed upon in the contract. This scenario has several options that can remedy the situation, but ultimately can become a hassle.

If a buyer finds themselves in this situation, the first thing to do is read over a bound copy of the financing contingency amendment in the bound contract. This document generally provides a framework to help deal with this situation and may state an amount that the property must appraise at in order for the purchaser to be locked in a contract. If the amount dictated in that section states a number higher than the valuation on the appraisal, then speak with the licensed real estate professional assisting you and they can help further.

One option the buyer may be presented with in this scenario is to pay the difference between the appraisal valuation and the agreed upon purchase price of the property in cash. While possible, I have personally not seen this happen frequently.

Another option on the table is that the buyer and seller renegotiate the contract. Certain things may be amended like closing costs provided, flooring allowances, and anything else written as a special stipulation to the contract. At this point, the overall goal of both parties is to close on the property at hand since there has been a lot of time, effort, and finances that have been put into the purchasing process so far.

Something else that may happen is that the buyer and seller may not agree on the negotiations presented in a revised contract and could potentially part ways. This scenario will require the agents, lenders, and brokerages involved in the transaction as well as both the buyers and sellers to determine how everything proceeds. If this scenario occurs, speak with the licensed real estate professional and licensed loan officer that have been assisting you throughout this process to provide guidance on how to proceed.

Notes on Repairs

If lender repairs are required based on the results of an appraisal, ensure that a *qualified*, licensed individual conducts the necessary repairs. This is imperative because the appraiser will be sent out to the property by the lender as many times as needed until the repairs have been conducted to the appraiser's satisfaction.

This is important to note as a buyer because every time an appraiser is sent back out to a property, it typically is an expense that the buyer will be responsible for paying. This is not the time to skimp on quality work, as it can quickly become quite a bit more expensive for a buyer to close on a particular property if the appraiser must be sent out to reinspect it frequently. For more information on repairs that need to be conducted and licensed contractors qualified to conduct the work, speak with the real estate professional that has been assisting you throughout the homebuying process.

Chapter Summary/Key Takeaways

- Quality is key!

- Read the contract

- Know who is liable for what

- When in doubt, talk it out

- Never let the deal die (unless you want it to!)

PART IV:

Making It Through the Homestretch

Chapter Nine:

The Final Walkthrough

The **final walkthrough** is the buyer's opportunity to view the property in its final form after all repairs have been completed. This is generally scheduled by the real estate professional assisting the buyer and is utilized for the buyer to see all the work that has been completed on the property prior to closing. This tends to be the final opportunity for any loose ends to be tied up and for any final reparations to be made, so look closely!

During the final walkthrough there are a lot of items to pay attention to and often not a lot of time. Because of this, you will need to methodical in your actions which will allow you to be quick but thorough. Prior to the final walkthrough, ensure to have a list of all repairs conducted assembled and easily accessible as well as something to take notes with. With the high likelihood of this being your last chance as a buyer to have any last-minute changes made, you must be as prepared as possible or risk missing something you may consider important.

The Five P's

Prior Preparation Prevents Poor Performance. Those are the Five P's to abide by in this phase of the purchasing process. The more prepared you are, the better off you will be. There is the possibility that a repair may have been conducted improperly or not at all with everything going on and the impending closing date looming overhead. Mistakes happen all the time. After all, humans are not perfect.

By properly preparing for the final walkthrough, you as a buyer have the ability to know exactly what to look for instead of wandering aimlessly around the house arguing with your significant other over where the pool table will go and what curtains would look best in the living room. There will be plenty of time for decorating the house later; for now you need to focus with the coming to an end in the near future.

Bring along the repair requests agreed upon as well as a copy of the home inspection and the appraisal, if you have access to it. Some of these documents typically include photos of various portions of the house. With sticky notes and something to write with, mark off the location of the item in question that was agreed upon for repairs and its corresponding photograph, and take note of the *exact* wording utilized in the amendment that addresses any concerns to the property. The wording on this document is absolutely crucial in my opinion, as it determines *exactly* what was to be conducted. If the document is vague and uses words like "upgrade", *do not* expect that it means that it will be replaced with something new.

For example, if it says, "upgrade the electrical breaker panel to code," the wording is up to the interpretation of the reader. In my opinion, if I saw that on a contract and represented the seller of a property, I would have a licensed electrician service and provide any upgrades necessary to the wiring and breakers inside the electrical panel. In no way, shape, or form would I interpret that to mean that my seller would be providing and paying for the labor to install a brand-new breaker panel because that *isn't* what was written in the contract.

Now the aforementioned example is provided to show the importance how word choice changes a minor repair that only costs a few hundred dollars to a major repair that can cost in the thousands. This shows that it is critical to understand the wording of the agreed upon repairs so you are completely aware of what to expect. As I like to say, "I like making things crystal clear so there aren't any hiccups at the end." In a business that works on fast timelines, everchanging markets, and consists of extremely large amounts of money on the line, it is important to ensure that all the t's are crossed and i's are dotted. Attention to detail is imperative, and that can be made easier by properly preparing for the final walkthrough.

At the Property

When you have arrived at the property, take a good look at everything on the exterior as well as the interior. Repairs are often conducted all over the property in various areas, and they are not always noticeable to an untrained eye. The difficulties that come with determining whether an item was required to be repaired is why it helps to be prepared prior to your arrival to the property.

As mentioned earlier when we discussed asking for the seller to conduct repairs, this again is a phase where you will want to be more concerned with the big-ticket items. Focus on items that historically are costly or could become a major issue to deal with at a later point. Quite frankly, if I have walked through the house with my client and the only thing that was missed was a drain stopper in a bathroom sink and the client complains about its absence, I will go out and purchase one for them in order to get the property to close. I urge you to look at the details, but please don't be petty. Trust in the abilities of the real estate professional assisting you and give them an opportunity to make things right.

How I Approach the Final Walkthrough

What I like to do during the final walkthrough of a property with my client is walk the exterior of the house twice; the first time looking exclusively at the roofline, chimney, gutters, and soffits; the second time looking at the siding, brick, mortar, fencing, foundation, yard, and anything else that needs attention. I do this because I do not want to miss seeing something important that may potentially require further attention by trying to evaluate too many items at once.

Once I am satisfied with what I have seen on the exterior of the property and have taken notes on anything that may need extra attention, I bring my client inside of the home and start the process room by room. After doing a once-over of the upper and the lower part of each room, I pull out my repairs list I prepared beforehand that states clearly with pictures what was supposed to be conducted and whether or not it was conducted to the agreed upon standard. I continue to do this room by room, checking everything in a timely manner to ensure that each repair was conducted, and the expected result was achieved.

Now, it is important to note that everyone has a different way of doing this process. The real estate professional that has been assisting you throughout your purchase process may have a different method, and that is completely fine. There are a thousand ways to skin a cat, and this is one of those scenarios. While I was serving as an Infantry Officer in the United States Army, my Commander had a saying he swore by. "Knecht," he'd say to me, "if it's stupid but it works, it ain't stupid."

As this quote so bluntly points out, a process is a process and as long as it functions and provides the desired results, the method involved in achieving those results isn't pertinent. I have seen people who always start from the top or the bottom of the house, in the kitchen, do all the bedrooms or bathrooms first, or even decide to begin in the attic. How they wish to complete this process is irrelevant, so long as they have a process and it allows them to ensure they have seen everything of concern.

What Happens If an Item Wasn't Repaired Correctly or At All?

If a repair that was agreed upon was not completed to the level stated in the contract (or worse, not at all), there are a few items that may occur. To start with, the real estate professional assisting you will take a look at whatever needs attention and will determine how minor or major the problem at hand is. If it happens to be a missing drain plug, light switch plate cover, or something of that nature on a relatively minor scale, your good agent most often will tell you that they'll take care of it and ensure to provide you with whatever is missing. They may even stop by the house and install it themselves after closing!

Should something be more than a minor inconvenience, or actually require a contractor to further work on the item, then things can become a little more detailed. After attempting to negotiate with the seller, it may be remedied via providing more in closing costs or a credit to the buyer for a contractor to come make the necessary repairs after the property closes. At this point, the last thing anyone wants is for closing to have to be rescheduled since the seller generally has moved out and the buyer needs to move in.

There are some rare occasions where the real estate professionals decide to work together and split the cost of the repair that needs to be conducted if they feel obligated to. This usually only happens when there is something that could have been conveyed inaccurately in the wording of the repair requests, if the property is in a higher price range, or the real estate professional feels that they may obtain more business through that particular client's referrals. Whatever the reason may be for this to occur, it is not something as a buyer to rely on. In most cases, the remedy is negotiated to the satisfaction of the buyer and the seller.

In the rare event that someone decides to obtain legal representation over an issue, the outcome is determined via a court of law. At any point in time throughout this process you are always welcome to speak to an attorney at your own expense. However, do not be surprised if the real estate professional you have been working with opts for all further communications to be conducted through their attorney if it comes down to this. For information on this process and how it may affect your specific scenario, seek legal counsel.

If everything has been determined to be satisfactory, or once all parties are satisfied with the final amendments that have been negotiated, it's time to head to closing!

Chapter Summary/Key Takeaways

- Prepare, prepare, prepare

- Look at the major things first

- Have a game plan

- Let the real estate professional help you

- It's okay to negotiate!

Chapter Ten:

What to Expect at the Closing Table

Picture this: after many weeks of repairs, packing, and excitement you have finally made it to the closing table! This is arguably the most highly anticipated part of the whole homebuying process. In mere minutes you will walk away with a smile on your face and keys in your hand to your new property! You are finally a homeowner!

Now that I have you dreaming about how you plan on redecorating for the most optimal fengshui, it is time to come back to reality. There are several things that still must be completed in order for you to get those keys and move on to greener pastures. Let's walk through the process, from beginning to end.

First Thing's First

I know that everyone likes to think of themselves as very busy individuals. People often show up late to appointments, take their time shopping, and seem to live on their own timelines. While there is nothing inherently wrong with that way of going about your daily routines, you will need to understand one thing and one thing only: for this portion of the process, you are *not* on your time. You are on the lawyer's time.

Lawyers are extremely busy, especially in real estate. As someone who works closely with them day in and day out, I have been granted the unique perspective that they are often booked down to as little as six-minute intervals. In essence, they have a lot on their plates.

Now this is where you as the buyer come into play. Because of how tightly knit a real estate lawyer's schedule typically tends to be, you need to be at their office *prepared* and *early*. If you are not, they generally will push reschedule your closing date and for the most part there isn't much you can do about it. Repeat this with me: *be prepared and be early.* You are on their time.

How do you come prepared? Simple. Show up to the attorney's office with at least two forms of government issued picture identification, a power of attorney if necessary, and anything else they may have asked you to complete. If you were required to wire funds to the closing, ensure that they were wired at least a day in advance so there aren't any hiccups with the transaction. I always recommend to my clients that they bring a checkbook with them to closing, as the final numbers may fluctuate slightly and many attorneys that I have worked with do not accept cash. Also, don't have your credit run until at least 24 hours after closing. This could potentially make the transaction not possible. For more information on this, speak with a licensed loan officer.

At the Table

After the attorney has called you into their office,
you will sit down and be presented a multitude of
documents. The one that typically is presented first to you
is known as the ALTA Statement. This is a document that
the attorney will go over with you line by line that states
the purchase price of the property, seller credits, taxes,
fees, and anything else that may be required. Essentially,
it is a breakdown of who pays for what in the transaction.
You will sign several copies of this document in blue ink
and pass it around the table so that everyone involved in
the transaction has an original copy.

If you have utilized a mortgage to obtain
financing, you will be signing a stack of documents
regarding the terms of the loan as well as the standard
documentation utilized in a cash transaction. While this is
just a brief overview, the attorney will explain to you each
document you are signing and what its purpose is. If you
utilized a mortgage, expect to be signing documents for
the better part of an hour.

After all documents have been signed, the attorney
will await confirmation of the wire transfer from the
lender and/or the buyer and will cut checks for all parties
involved in the transaction that are due any payment.
From there, you get the keys to the property along with
your copy of the documents that you signed, take a photo,
and part ways to start moving in!

After the Closing

After closing has been conducted and you are the owner of the house, you are able to turn on utilities and apply for a homestead exemption if applicable. The real estate professional that you worked with can provide you with more information about how to go about doing that for your specific property.

If for whatever reason there are issues that occur to the property that you need assistance with, feel free to give the real estate professional that you worked with a call. If you have a home warranty, use it! If not, or it isn't covered under your home warranty, most real estate professionals would be happy to pass on a contact of theirs that may be able to provide the service that you require assistance with. However, do not expect for that real estate professional to pay for the work that you need conducted on your home nor should you call them every time something happens to your property that needs fixing. Unless they are a property manager that you are paying to manage your home, their role in your homebuying process is complete once the transaction has closed in the majority of cases. After that, anything a real estate professional does on your behalf to assist you is out of the goodness of their heart.

Houses are wonderful, but they also are a responsibility. Things break and need to be replaced; it is the nature of the beast. While rare, I have heard of people having a pipe burst a few days after closing or a problem

77

with the water heater, HVAC system, refrigerator, etc.... The list is endless. And that generally does not mean that the real estate professional that you worked with is at fault for this occurring. In most cases, they are sorry to hear that something broke and are glad to help get you in touch with someone to get it fixed or instruct you on how your home warranty can help, but this is something that happens and is generally not their financial liability. You purchased the house, and you are the one responsible for maintaining it.

That was not intended to scare you off from purchasing a home. Merely it is something that you must understand that when purchasing a home, and by default entering homeownership, there is a more active role in maintaining your residence than if you were living in an apartment complex. In your home, you make the rules. Want to have three dogs? Go for it. Want to paint the bathrooms pink? Have fun. Want to leave your Christmas lights up all year? Tacky, but nobody can stop you (unless you have a HOA).

The bottom line is that owning your own home is a blessing. While owning a home is something you must embrace the responsibility of as it requires a more active role in your life, it also allows you freedom and independence in ways you may have never experienced before. There is a reason why so many people in the United States and around the world work so hard to attain this dream. And soon, you will be joining their ranks and reaping the rewards of homeownership.

Chapter Summary/Key Takeaways

- Prepare and be early

- Understand what you are signing

- Ask for help if necessary

- Things break, it happens

- Enjoy your new home!

Knecht/The Real Estate Buyer's Guide to Buying A House

Epilogue

As I said in the beginning and I will repeat again now, this book is intended to act as a guide to help elevate your understanding of the process of buying your first home. While it does not nor will it ever cover all scenarios you may encounter in your specific transaction, I wrote it as a way to provide you with the framework of the homebuying process and what you can expect so that you can prepare accordingly and "be in the know."

Writing this book is very important to me because I often work with first-time home buyers who do not know anything about the process that they are about to find themselves in. There are many individuals that I come across in this industry that simply think that buying a house is akin to purchasing groceries. If they like it, they pay on the spot, and it's theirs.

This book proves to be an educational resource for anyone considering purchasing a property to have something to prepare themselves with. From start to finish, you have learned everything from how to find a real estate professional that will be the best fit for you to what you need to know when it is time to ask for repairs, and everything in between. You now have a firm grasp of how to approach the path to homeownership that lays ahead of you.

From the very bottom of my heart, I hope that this has helped you gain a greater understanding of what it takes to purchase your first home and help jumpstart your path to homeownership. I believe that there is nothing greater than having a place to call your own, and it is my passion to assist others in obtaining the joys of homeownership.

I wish you the best of luck on the amazing journey that lays ahead of you! And remember: the more prepared you are, the better off you will be. Enjoy the process, it will be over before you know it. And don't forget, utilize this information to "Connect You to Your Dream Home!"©

Very respectfully,

Cal Knecht

Realtor®

GRI®, ABR®, SRS®, MRP®, SFR®, B.A.

Glossary

Agency- the formal relationship a potential buyer/seller has with a real estate professional.

Appraisal- a document requested by a bank or lender which dictates the perceived value of a specific property.

Appraiser- a licensed individual sent by the lender or bank to check a specific property for various hazards, code violations, and necessary repairs in order to help the lender guaranty the loan.

Closing- when ownership of a property is transferred from a seller to a buyer at an attorney's office.

Closing costs- items required to be paid in order for the mortgage to be obtained and the attorney to transfer ownership of the property from the seller to the buyer.

Comparative Market Analysis- a report that compares a specific subject property to other properties within a close proximity to the subject that have sold recently.

Designated Agent- an agent that is assigned to work with you to protect your interests.

Dual Agency- a situation where the buyer and seller are represented by the same agent.

Due Diligence- the timeframe in a real estate contract that a buyer is allowed to conduct inspections on the property and gather any and all information that the buyer deems necessary in order to help them make a more educated purchase.

Earnest Money- a deposit made by a buyer which is used as collateral to secure a property. The amount is negotiable.

Final Walkthrough- the buyer's opportunity to view the property in its final form after all repairs have been completed.

Offer- A written agreement stating that a buyer would wish to purchase a property for a set price under certain conditions that are to be negotiated.

Appendix A

Wants	Needs

Knecht/The Real Estate Buyer's Guide to Buying A House

Appendix B

Cost Analysis

Monthly Budget:	$
Monthly Mortgage Payment Principal:	$
PMI:	$
Taxes:	$
Homeowners Insurance:	$
Other Insurance:	$
Other Expenses:	$
Total Monthly Cost:	$

Acknowledgments

I want to say a special thank you to my wife, Arrí, and my son Alonzo for their never-ending patience, support, and commitment. I cannot express in words how much the two of you mean to me, and I love you both with all of my heart.

I want to thank Ricki Lynn Cook for opening my eyes to the world of real estate and for pointing me in the right direction. For this, I cannot thank you enough.

I want to thank my parents and brothers for teaching me resilience and how to never give up when life gets you down, and to always get back up and find a way to make it work.

I want to thank GOD for looking out for me and my family through thick and thin, and for always being there for us no matter how bleak things may seem.

I want to thank my cousin Elias, my grandfather Francis, and my grandmother Anita for always watching over me from heaven above. May you rest in peace.

I want to thank all who have read this book, may this information help you on your journey to homeownership.

I want to thank all of my past clients for trusting in me and allowing me the opportunity to serve them while taking care of their real estate needs.

And last but not least, I want to thank my family, my friends, mentors, fellow veterans, and everyone else who assisted me in any way.

Without all of you, I would have never made it to where I currently am today.

Thank you all for everything you have provided me with. GOD Bless.

About the Author

Cal Knecht is currently a licensed real estate agent in the states of Georgia (license #389218) and Alabama (license #000122692). He holds the designation of Graduate, REALTOR® Institute, which requires over 120 hours of continuing education, transactions completed, and sales volume among other requirements in addition to obtaining and maintaining licensure. Cal also holds the designations of Accredited Buyer's Representative®, Seller Representative Specialist®, Military Relocation Specialist®, and Short Sales and Foreclosure Resource®. These designations have allowed Cal to serve his clients with excellence while helping to protect their investment.

Prior to being a real estate professional, Cal was an Infantry Officer in the United States Army. After a parachute malfunction, Cal medically retired at the rank of First Lieutenant. Cal is a graduate of the University of Connecticut with a Bachelor of Arts in Latino and Latin American Studies.

Cal currently lives in Phenix City, Alabama close to Fort Benning with his wife, son, and three dogs. Cal enjoys volunteering and assisting other veterans in the community as well as watching sports, playing with his son, and researching potential investment properties. He also likes to speak publicly and teach others how they too can begin investing in real estate.

Cal has sold many millions of dollars' worth of properties in his tenure in real estate through countless transactions. His passion for writing this book was to provide potential homebuyers insights on what to expect and be aware of throughout the process of purchasing property.

Cal is always happy to speak with interested parties to help any questions that they may have about the homebuying experience, and can be reached at calknechtenterprises@gmail.com. You can also visit www.calknechtenterprises.com to learn more about upcoming speaking engagements, noteworthy events, search for properties, and to calculate your potential mortgage payment.

Knecht/The Real Estate Buyer's Guide to Buying A House

Knecht/The Real Estate Buyer's Guide to Buying A
House